Eric James

Visit this author's website for more books & journals:
ericjames.co.uk

This December 20______

write the year here

Journal
Belongs to:

____

Aged:

____

WELCOME!

This is your very own
Christmas Journal!

Each day you'll get a little rhyme and an activity. But most importantly we'll give you a bit of space to write down things that have happened (as well as any interesting thoughts you've had).

Journals are fun to keep and even more fun to read again when you're a little older, so use it to keep track of all the brilliant things that happen this Christmas!

December 1st

On the <u>FIRST</u> day of December
Santa writes a GREAT BIG LIST.
There's lots and lots to do this month,
and NOTHING can be missed.

He jots down 'buy some carrots',
Then he scribbles 'clean the sleigh'.
'This list will be quite long,' he laughs.
'I might be here all day!'

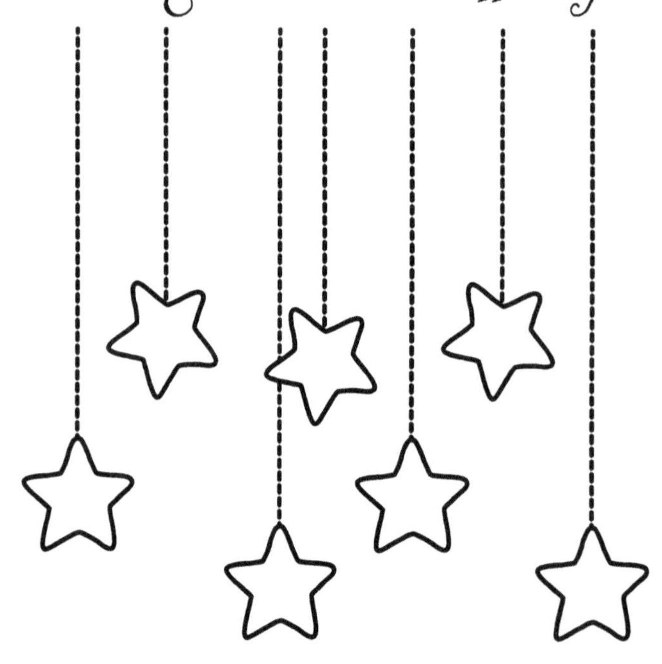

Activity

Talking of lists, what are your top 5 presents? If Christmas Day hasn't arrived yet, write down the presents you are hoping to get. Or, if you've received this book for Christmas Day, write down the 5 best presents you were given (surely this book is one of them!)

1 ....

2 ....

3 ....

4 ....

5 ....

Journal Page

Today

Santa spent the first day of December listing all the tasks that need doing before Christmas Day. Lists are brilliant when you have lots of things to do and you want to make sure you don't forget to do any of them!

I wonder what Santa will get up to tomorrow!

December 2nd

On the 2nd of December
Santa goes to check the mail.
He gets ten sacks of letters
every hour without fail.

He searches through the massive pile
And gets down on all fours.
I think he's double-checking
Whether one of them is YOURS!

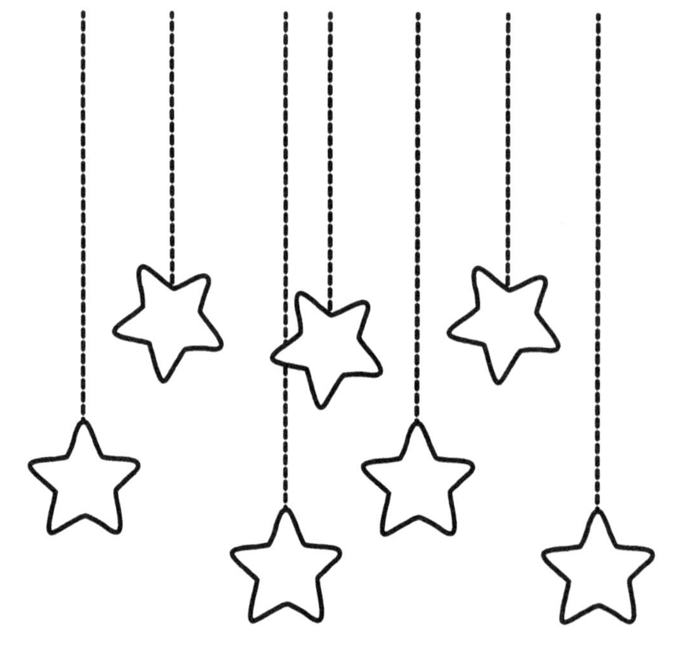

Activity

Have you written your letter to Santa yet? If you have then use the journal page to plan your thank you letter!

Dear Santa,

my name is ______________________________

I have been a really good child this year. The kindest thing I have done is ______________________________

____

For Christmas I would really like

____

____

____

____

All my love,

____

Journal Page

Today

Today Santa checked to see if your letter had arrived.

He's very good at knowing what you want even if you don't send him a letter, but I prefer not to leave it to chance!

I wonder what Santa will get up to tomorrow!

December 3rd

On the THIRD day of December
Santa checks the factory shelves.
He watches as they start to fill
With presents made by elves.

He wears a pair of headphones
(Elves can make a LOT of noise!)
They laugh and whoop and giggle
While they're making all those toys!

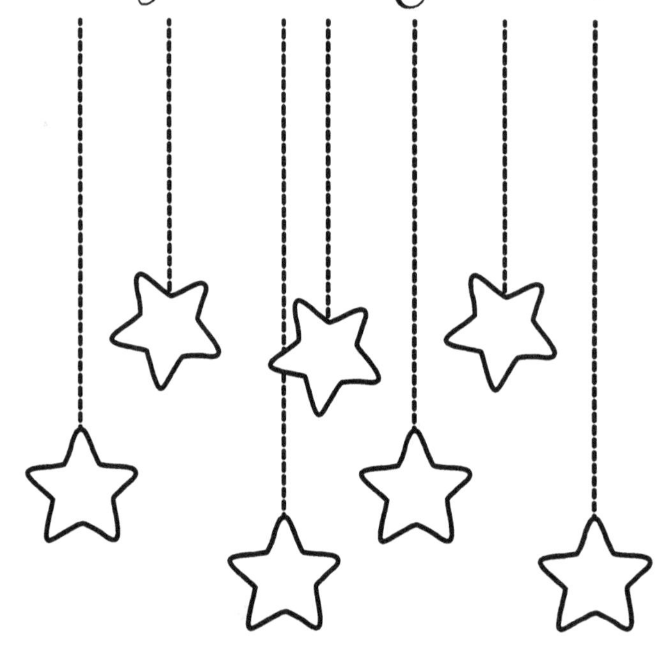

Activity

How colorful can you make this elf ?

I've not put anything important on this page.
That's because it follows a coloring activity.
If the colors show through the paper, it won't
matter as much :)

Parents: this occasionally means a slight tweak
to the order in which the pages appear.

Journal Page

Today

Today Santa checked the shelves in The Toy Factory to see how the toy production is coming along. It's important to make sure that everything is on track for Christmas.

Santa and his team of elves make billions of toys every year. No one knows exactly how many elves work in The Toy Factory, but we know they must work very quickly in order to make that many!

I wonder what Santa will get up to tomorrow!

December 4th

On the FOURTH day of December
Santa checks his Santa Hat.
The pompom's almost falling off!
'We can't be having that.'

Mrs Claus gets out some thread.
She knows just what to do.
She sews it back on tightly.
Now the hat's as good as new.

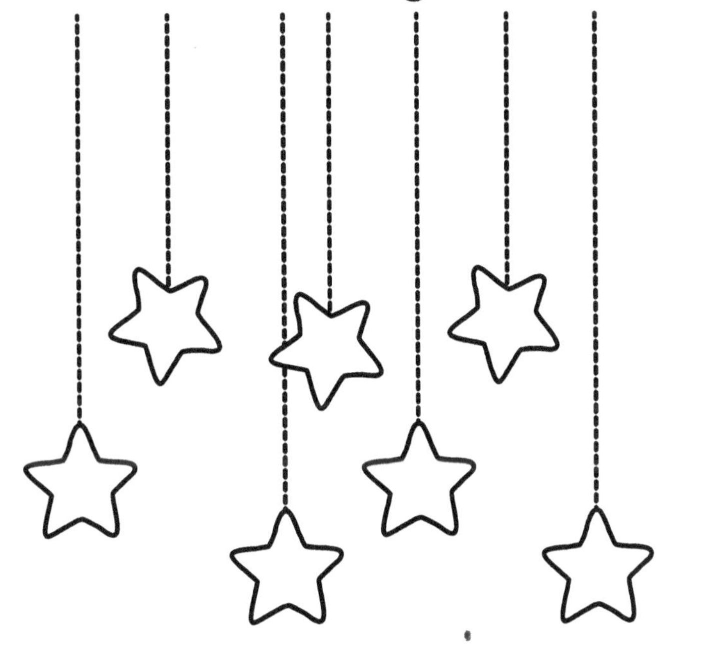

Activity

CHRISTMAS SCRAMBLE 1

Two cheeky elves thought it would be funny to mix up all the letters in these Christmas words. Can you unscramble them for me?

You'll find the answers at the back of the book.

ATNSA

EERT

SGFIT

OWSN

Journal Page

Today

Today Santa checked his uniform to make sure it's ready for the big day. He noticed that the pompom on his hat was almost falling off. Luckily Mrs Claus has excellent sewing skills.

What is your Christmas Day outfit?

I wonder what Santa will get up to tomorrow!

December 5th

On the FIFTH day of December
Mrs Claus whips up a cake.
She leaves it on the window sill
And wow, it's smelling great!

The smell attracts a group of elves
Who stand outside and stare.
She wags her finger at the group
And says 'ELVES, DON'T YOU DARE!'

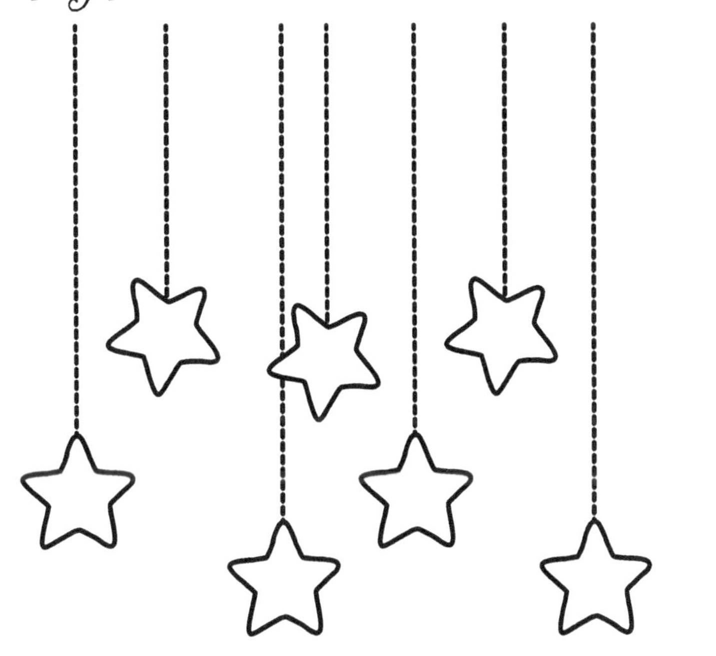

Activity

If you could design your dream cake (or cookie), what ingredients would you put in it? Chocolate? Marshmallows? Broccoli? An old shoe?

Describe it below:

Journal Page

Today

Today Mrs Claus baked a Christmas cake. She had to make sure the hungry elves didn't gobble it all up!
(I'm sure she'll let them have some, eventually).

In many countries, especially countries with colder climates, traditional festive desserts are often made with dried fruit; examples include Christmas cake, Christmas pudding and mince pies - these last two are often served hot, with cream or Creme Anglais (a custard sauce).

I wonder what Santa will get up to tomorrow!

December 6th

On the SIXTH day of December
Santa heads out on his sleigh.
He comes back with a pine tree
Shouting 'Decorate away!'

The elves come rushing out to see.
Delighted at the sight,
They make the tree look wonderful
With candy canes and lights.

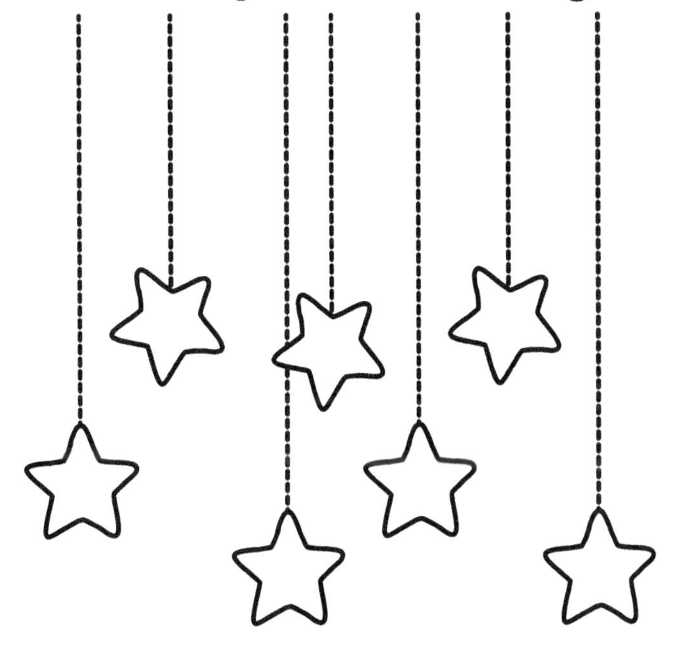

Journal Page

Activity

Have you put up your Christmas tree yet? Draw a picture of it (or if you haven't put one up yet, draw what you *think* it will look like):

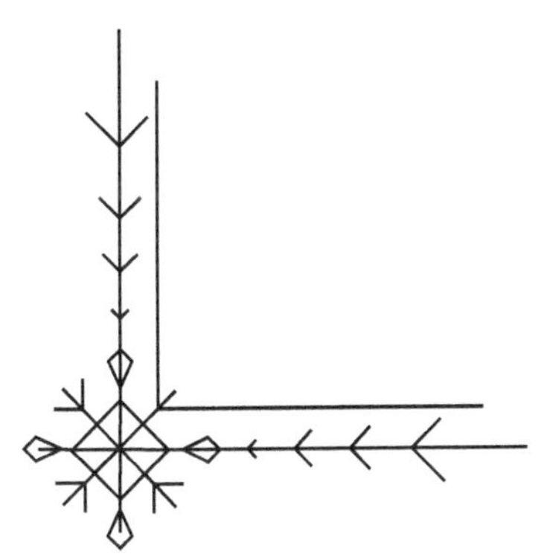

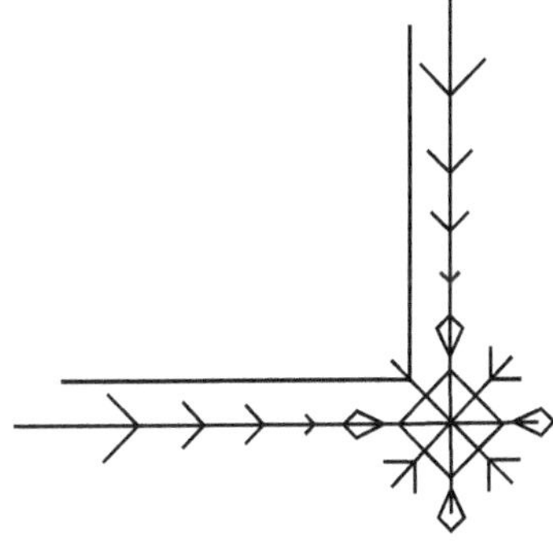

I've not put anything important on this page. That's because it follows a coloring activity. If the colors show through the paper, it won't matter as much :)

Parents: this occasionally means a slight tweak to the order in which the pages appear.

Today

Today Santa brought home a Christmas tree and all the elves in the village came out to decorate it with candy canes and lights.

There are certain tree-types that are regularly used for Christmas trees. The most popular types are Pine, Fir and Spruce. They are all evergreens, which means they don't shed their leaves (or needles) in the winter.

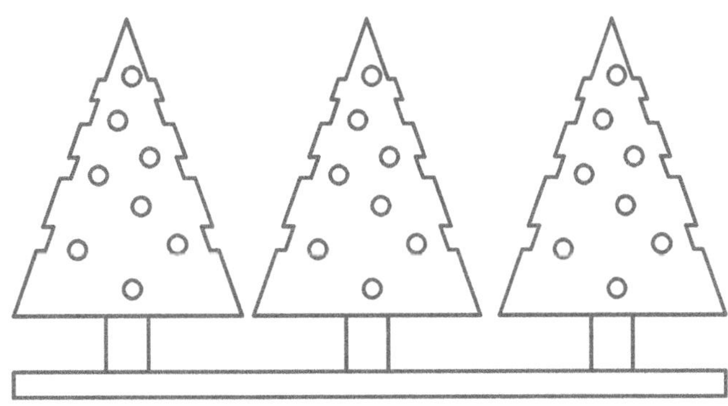

I wonder what Santa will get up to tomorrow!

December 7th

On the 7th of December
Mrs Claus serves her dessert.
Santa eats three portions.
'Just one more? It wouldn't hurt!'

His wife shouts 'Naughty Santa!'
And she takes his bowl away.
'Eat too much and you will never
Fit inside your sleigh!'

She puts the rest upon a plate
And shouts out to the elves
'I've got dessert for you to eat.
Come quickly! Help yourselves!'

Activity

Can you help the penguin find its way through the maze and get to the room filled with presents?

Find the answer at the back of the book

Journal Page

Today

Today Santa and the elves enjoyed some of Mrs Claus' Christmas dessert, and Santa had one portion too many!

Earlier on I mentioned 'mince pies'. These are pies filled with 'mincemeat' ... but eaten as *a dessert!* Yuck.

However, it's not as disgusting as it sounds. This type of 'mincemeat' is actually made from chopped fruit and spices. 'Mince' means to chop finely, and a very, very long time ago the word 'meat' referred to food in general, not just food made from animals. Whew! That's okay then.

I wonder what Santa will get up to tomorrow!

December 8th

On the EIGHTH day of December
Santa says 'Elf Engineers,
I'd love it if you'd make my sleigh
MUCH SPEEDIER this year!'

The engineers look thoughtful
As they work out what to do.
They nod their heads and all agree
It'll take a day or two!

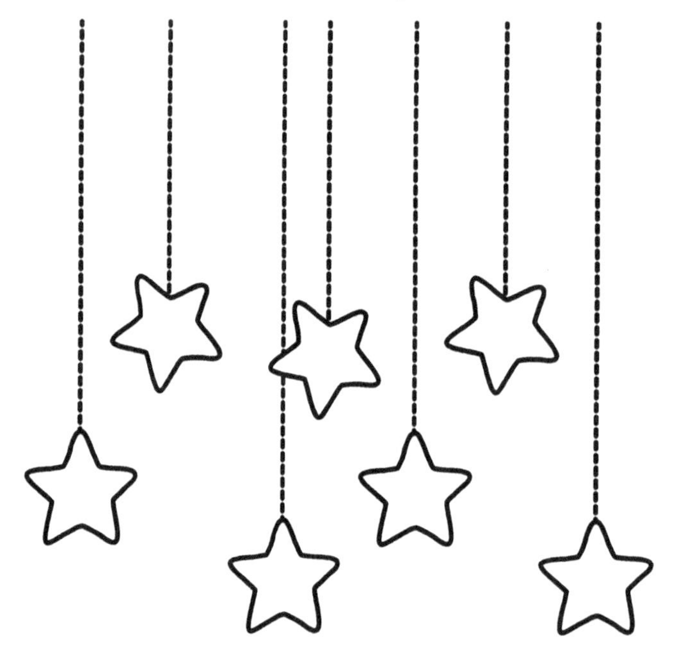

Activity

People love telling jokes at Christmas. Tell these jokes to your friends and family, and see if they laugh or groan:

JOKE: A snowman was seen in a supermarket buying a carrot. Why was he embarrassed?
ANSWER: Because no one likes getting caught picking their nose.

JOKE: Why does a broken drum make such a great Christmas present?
ANSWER: It can't be beaten.

JOKE: What do you get if you cross a bell with a skunk?
ANSWER: Jingle smells.

Journal Page

Today

Today Santa asked the elves to work on his sleigh to make it fly even faster (and it's already very fast!)

Name 3 things you think they could do to it, to make it faster:

I wonder what Santa will get up to tomorrow!

December 9th

On the NINTH day of December
Santa starts to plan his flight.
He's got a rather massive map.
It's really quite a sight!

It takes up half the sitting room
When laid out on the floor,
But it helps him plan a nice fast route
He's never flown before.

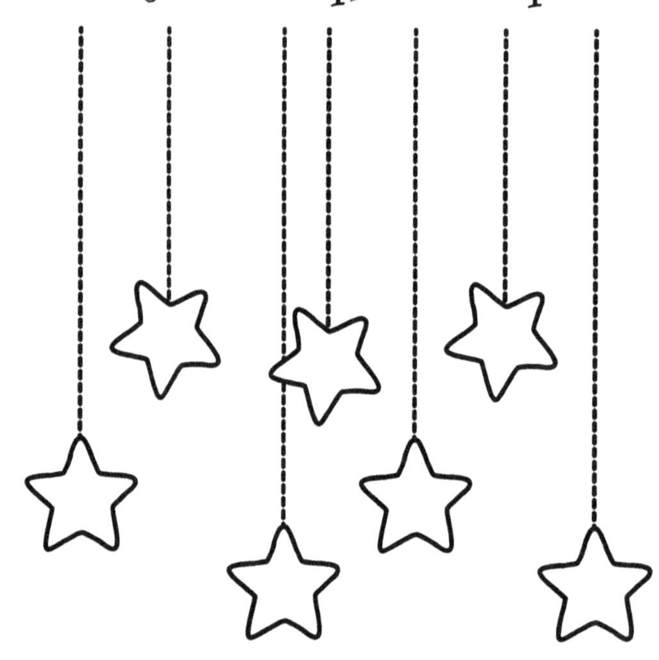

Activity

Tongue-twisters are groups of words that are tricky to say, but also fun to try saying fast.

Can you say this tongue-twister 10 times really quickly without stopping?

Santa's snow shoes were super-snuggly

Practice it a few times and then challenge everyone else you live with, to see who can say it the fastest.

Journal Page

Today

Today Santa planned the route he will travel on Christmas Eve. Every year there are more and more children to deliver to, so he wants to have the fastest sleigh and plan the quickest route.

Part of the reason Santa can travel all around the world in a single night is because of something called 'time-zones'. When it's morning or afternoon in some countries it is night-time in other countries. How crazy is that!

I wonder what Santa will get up to tomorrow!

December 10th

On the TENTH day of December
Santa's engineers reply:
'We've added ROCKETS to your sleigh.
Come out and watch it fly!'

It takes off rather nicely,
Loops-the-loop and sweeps around.
But then it starts to wobble
And it crash-lands on the ground!

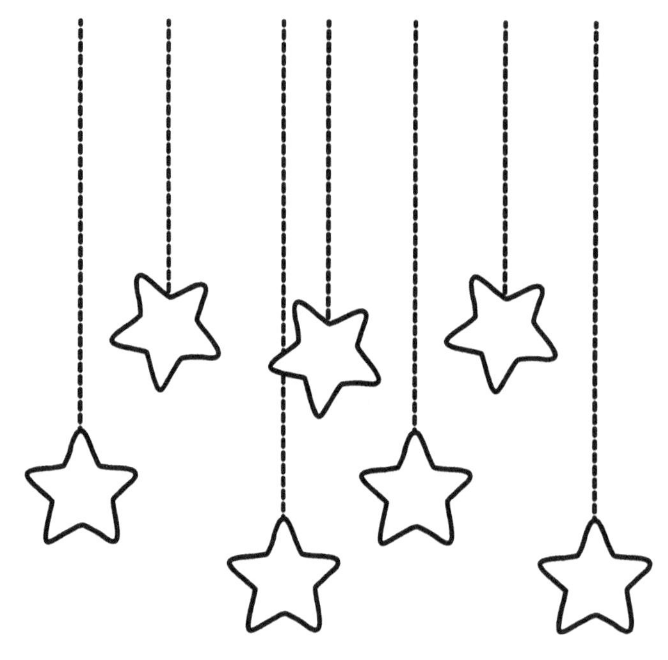

Activity

Find the following hidden words in the grid below (they could be written in any direction):

santa, snowball, penguins, ginger, presents, ice, snowflake, scarf, tree

A	S	J	E	R	E	G	N	I	G
S	F	N	E	S	C	A	R	F	W
N	S	E	O	H	R	U	S	Y	P
O	A	R	E	W	K	J	S	R	R
W	N	J	T	H	B	U	S	Y	E
F	T	G	R	B	F	A	S	T	S
L	A	J	E	F	W	U	L	Y	E
A	D	R	E	I	C	E	S	L	N
K	S	J	C	H	S	W	S	C	T
E	E	P	E	N	G	U	I	N	S

(Answers at the back of the book)

Journal Page

Today

Today the elves finished working on Santa's sleigh, but oh-dear, it seems like there was a bit of a problem with the rockets!

It's okay though - nobody was hurt, and the elves are very good at rebuilding things. Perhaps next time they'll use smaller rockets!

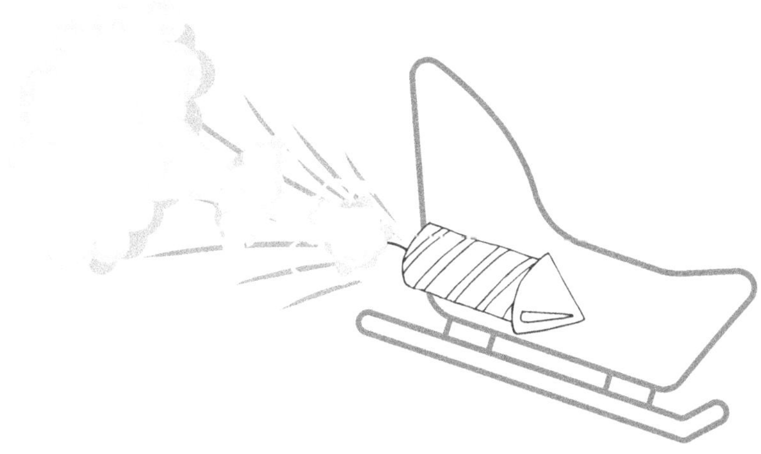

I wonder what Santa will get up to tomorrow!

December 11th

On the 11th of December
Santa wakes up at first light.

He sees the fresh snow on the ground
And shouts out 'SNOWBALL FIGHT!'

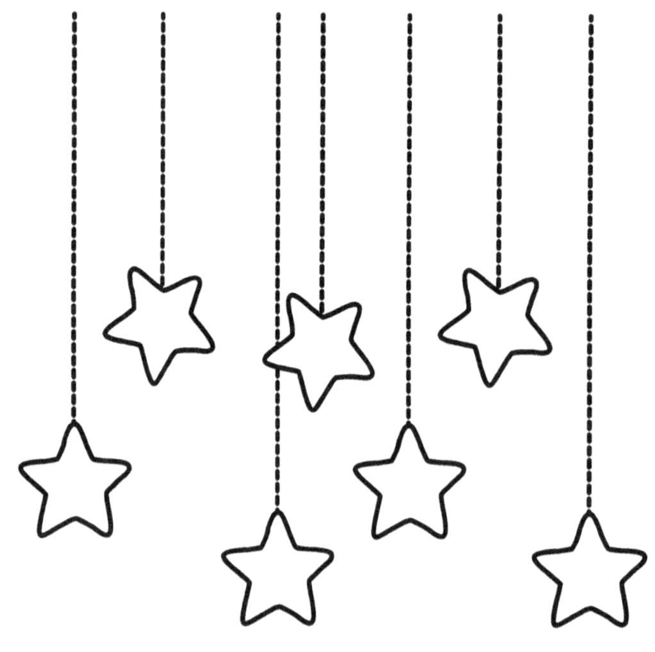

Activity

These pictures are not the same. How many differences can you spot?

(Answers at the back of the book)

Journal Page

Today

Today Santa and the elves had a snowball fight. Who would you challenge to a snowball fight and who do you think would win?

If you keep rolling a snowball on the ground it could turn into the start of a snow person. The record for the biggest snow person in the world belongs to residents of Bethel, Maine, USA, and surrounding towns.

13 *million* pounds of snow were used to build Olympia, the snow woman. She was only a few feet shorter than the Statue of Liberty!

I wonder what Santa will get up to tomorrow!

December 12th

On the TWELFTH day of December
Mrs Claus makes egg and beans,
But Santa gets it on his suit.
It'll have to be steam-cleaned!

'Messy pup,' says Mrs Claus.
'You need to take more care!
I'll take your suit for cleaning,
But what ARE you going to wear?'

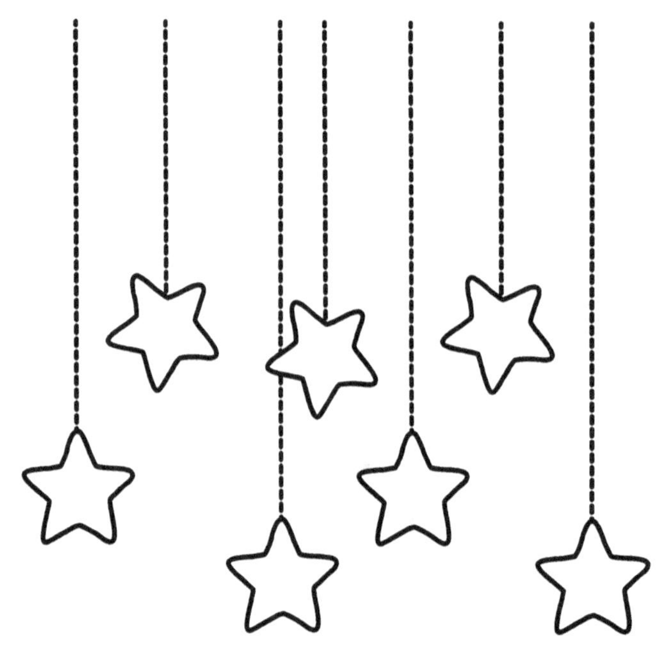

Activity

Color the scene. Perhaps draw in some people having a snowball fight!

I've not put anything important on this page. That's because it follows a coloring activity. If the colors show through the paper, it won't matter as much :)

Parents: this occasionally means a slight tweak to the order in which the pages appear.

Journal Page

Today

Today Santa had to have his Santa suit taken to the cleaners after spilling egg and beans down it.

What do you think Santa wears when he is not in his big, red suit? Perhaps you'll find out tomorrow!

I wonder what Santa will get up to tomorrow!

December 13th

On the 13th of December
Santa's in BERMUDA SHORTS!
He strokes his big white beard
while reading
Through the Elf Reports ...

They tell him who's been naughty
And they tell him who's been nice.
Your name is on the Nice List
And they've underlined it TWICE!

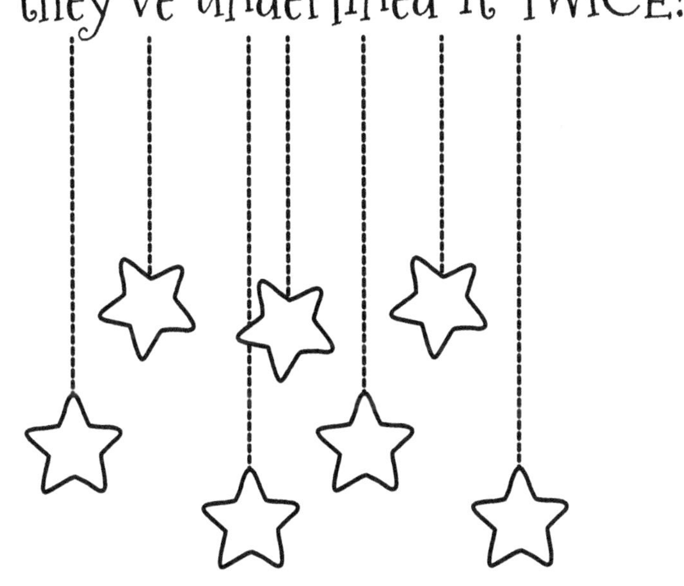

Activity

Elf reports? Oh that reminds me, your activity today is to do *at least* one REALLY NICE thing for the people you live with.

I'm sure you're already very good, but why not do something extra-nice today? You never know, the elves might be watching and could report your good deeds back to Santa!

Don't forget to write about your good deeds in your journal when you've done them. For now you can start by writing down 3 quick ideas. What type of good deeds could you do?

1 ....

2 ....

Journal Page

Today

Today Santa's job was to check through the Elf Reports in order to see who has been naughty and who has been nice.

What good things do you think the elves say about you?

I wonder what Santa will get up to tomorrow!

December 14th

On the 14th of December
Santa hears about the sleigh.
'We've fixed it up. We'll fly again.
Come out and watch today.'

It takes off rather nicely,
And it whizzes through the night.
Santa's clapping loudly.
Well done elves! You got it right!

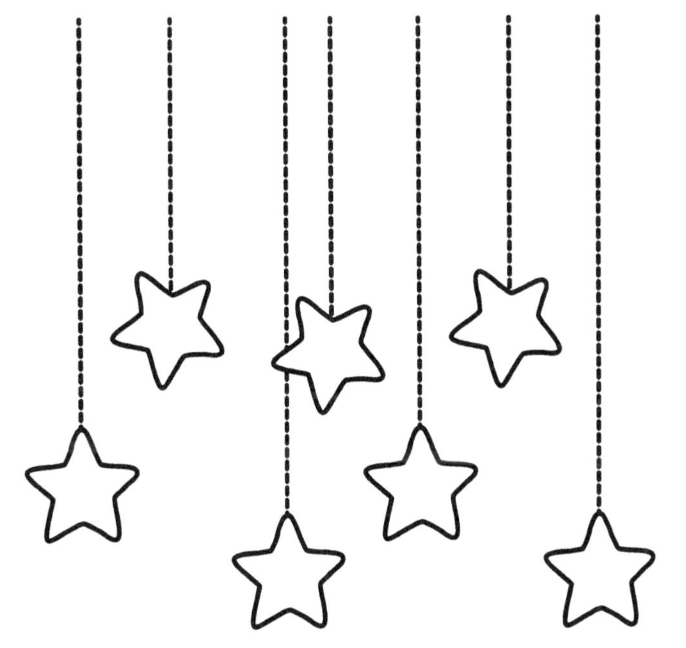

Activity

Join the dots:

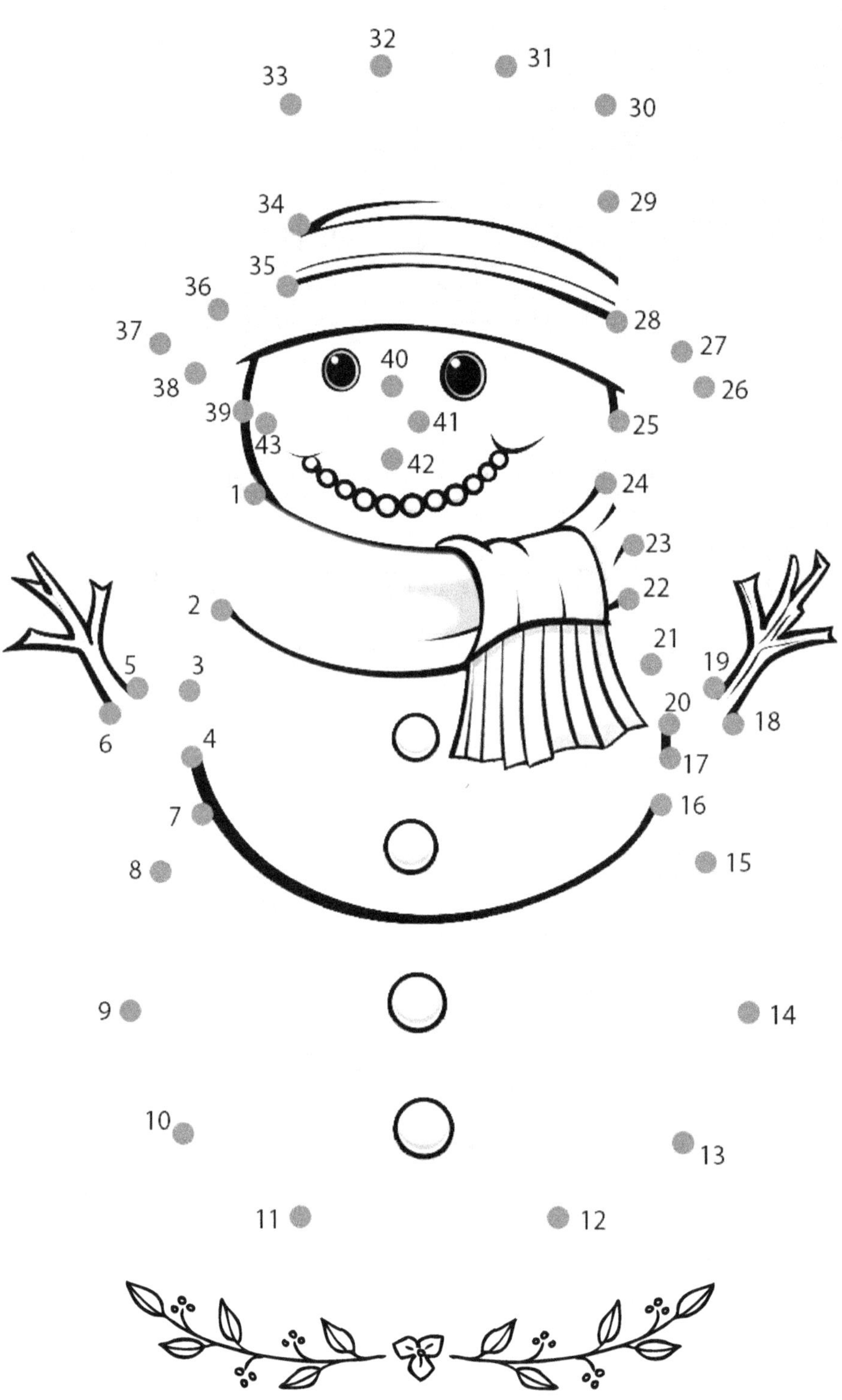

Journal Page

Today

Today the elves finally got the sleigh working. Santa is really happy because it's nice and speedy. In fact it's the fastest vehicle ever ...

On Christmas Eve Santa has roughly 31 hours to visit every child (thanks to time-zone differences) and there are about 640 million stops to make. That means he has to make about 20.5 million stops every hour! **Speedy indeedy!**

I wonder what Santa will get up to tomorrow!

December 15th

On the 15th of December
Santa has his suit returned.
He dresses,
then eats Sloppy Joes!
No lessons have been learned.

'Listen here,' says Mrs Claus,
'Tonight we eat spare ribs.
I'll only let you have some
If you wear your Santa bib!'

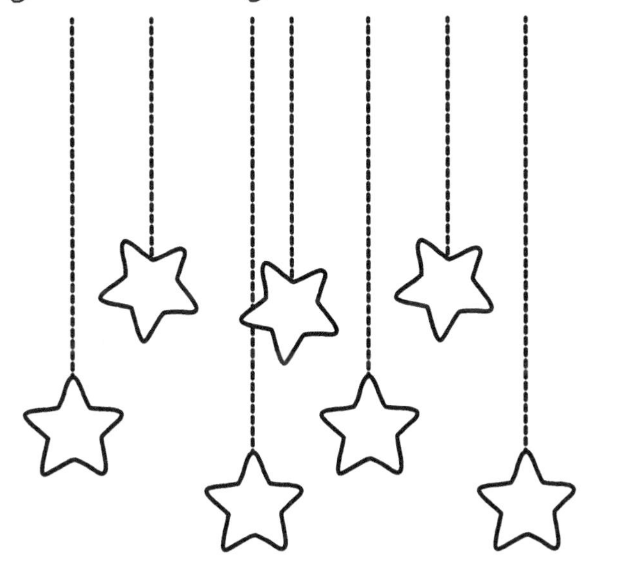

Activity

CHRISTMAS QUIZ

Can you answer these festive questions?
(Find the answers at the back of the book)

Q1:
How many reindeer does Santa have?

Q2:
Where does Santa live?

Q3:
What color is the Grinch?

Q4:
What is Rudolf's favorite food?

Q5:
What type of calendar do we use to count down to Christmas?

Journal Page

Today

Today Santa got his suit back from the cleaners, but it isn't long before he risks getting it dirty again!

Santa *loves* his food. He makes about 640 million stops on Christmas Eve. If he eats and drinks everything left out for him he will consume a total of 150 *billion* calories. That's food for thought!

I wonder what Santa will get up to tomorrow!

December 16th

On the 16th of December
Santa polishes the sleigh.
Each sleigh bell has to tinkle
in EXACTLY the right way.

The bells tell everybody that
He's flying overhead,
So any children still awake
Can make sure they're in bed!

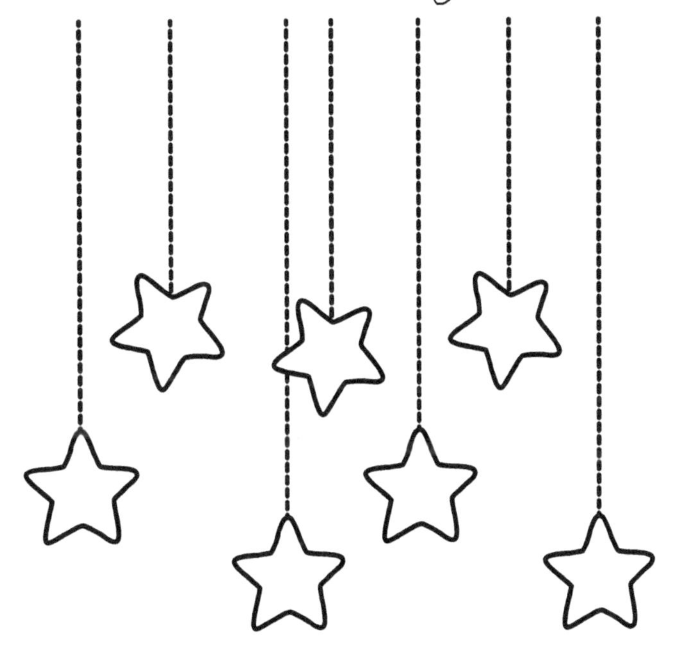

Activity

Everyone loves a good Christmas song!
Can you make up a song and sing it to your family?

Perhaps you can base it on an existing song or carol. Here's one that Elfis the Elf started writing to the tune of 'Good King Wenceslas':

♪ ♩ ♫ ♬

Elfis loves his pizzas cooked
Deep and crisp and even.
But he doesn't eat the crusts.
Those bits he'll be leavin'

♪ ♩ ♫ ♬

Now it's your turn:

Journal Page

Today

Sleigh bells are considered to be ***the*** sound of Christmas! Listen to popular Christmas songs closely, you'll hear the sound of these little ball-shaped bells in the background of almost all of them.

And of course there is even a song called 'Jingle Bells'. We associate this song with Christmas but it was actually written to celebrate Thanksgiving.

I wonder what Santa will get up to tomorrow!

December 17th

On the 17th of December
The elves sing festive tunes.
They crowd beneath the Christmas tree
And sing all afternoon.

The youngest elves are giggling
As Santa sings along.
He usually gets the NOTES correct
But gets the WORDS all wrong!

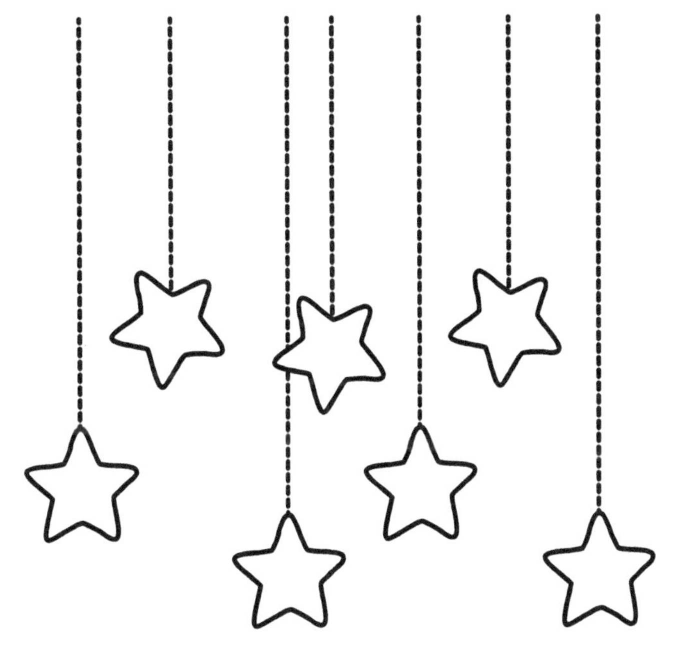

Activity

Here's a picture of Santa singing. The 2 versions are not the same. Can you spot all the differences?

Find the answers at the back of the book

Journal Page

Today

Today Santa and the elves had a bit of a sing-song around the Christmas tree.

The biggest-selling Christmas song of all time is 'White Christmas', sung by an American actor called Bing Crosby.

Why his parents named him after the sound that the microwave makes when it's finished cooking, we'll never know!

I wonder what Santa will get up to tomorrow!

December 18th

On the 18th of December
Santa brushes down his suit.
He shines his big belt buckle
And he polishes his boots.

He trims his big white whiskers
And he gets his trousers pressed.
Christmas Day is almost here.
He wants to look his best!

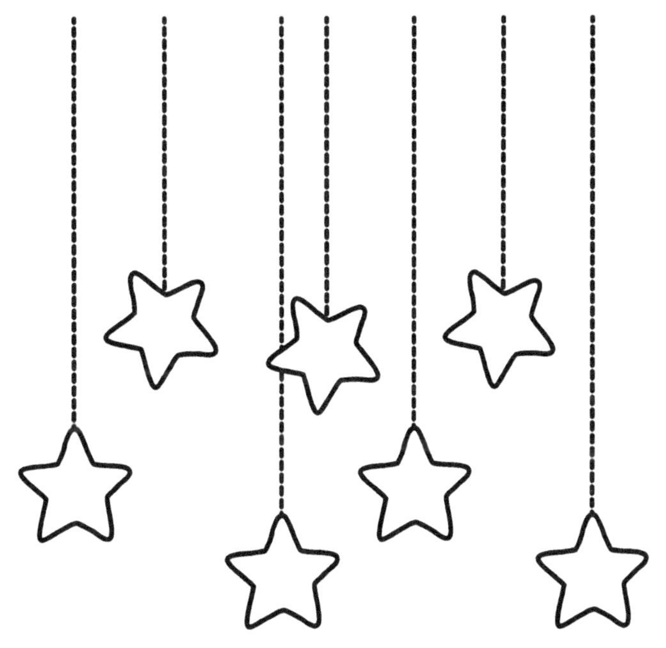

Journal Page

Activity

Color the picture!

I've not put anything important on this page.
that's because it follows a coloring activity.
If the colors show through the paper, it won't
matter as much :)

Parents: this occasionally means a slight tweak
to the order in which the pages appear.

Today

Today Santa tidied himself up for the big day.

Wearing a Christmas sweater always puts me in the Christmas spirit. Some countries have a 'Christmas Sweater Day' or even an 'Ugliest Sweater Day': a day on which you are encouraged to wear a Christmas sweater - perhaps the most embarrassing one you can find - to work or school, and in return you donate a little money to charity.

Have you got a Christmas sweater? If so, what's on it?

I wonder what Santa will get up to tomorrow!

December 19th

On the 19th of December
Posters go up everywhere:
'It's Movie Night at Santa's House.
I'd love to see you there!'

The young elves are excited
When they see the GREAT BIG SCREEN.
They watch the movie 'Home Alone'
While munching on ice cream.

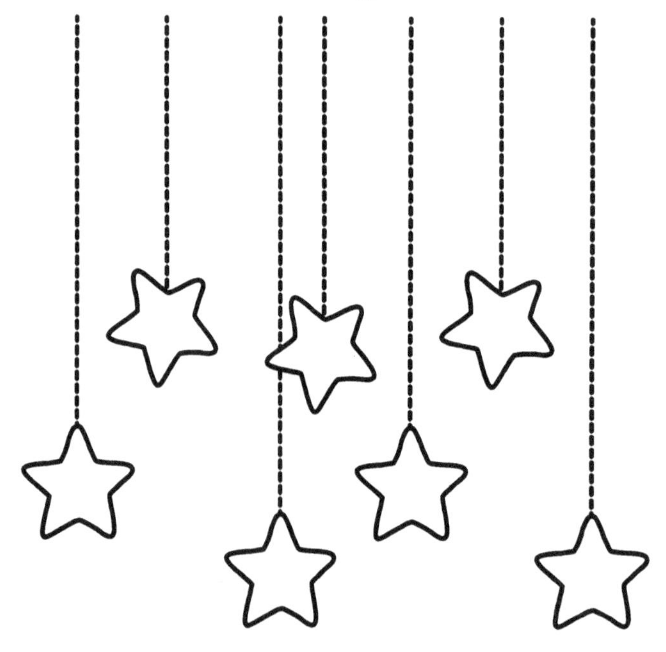

Activity

How did you get on with the last tongue-twister?
Would you like another one?

Say this one 10 times, really quickly without stopping:

Eleven elves eat every ice cream eagerly

Journal Page

Today

Today Santa invited everyone in the village to watch a Christmas movie.

The Christmas movie that has made the most money at the cinema is ‘The Grinch’, followed by ‘Home Alone’.

What’s your favorite Christmas movie, and why?

I wonder what Santa will get up to tomorrow!

December 20th

On the 20th of December
Santa's phone receives a call.
'Can you come round to our house?
Elfis Elf can't sleep at all!'

The young elf's SO EXCITED.
He's not slept for several days,
So Santa reads him stories.
Now they're BOTH snoring away.

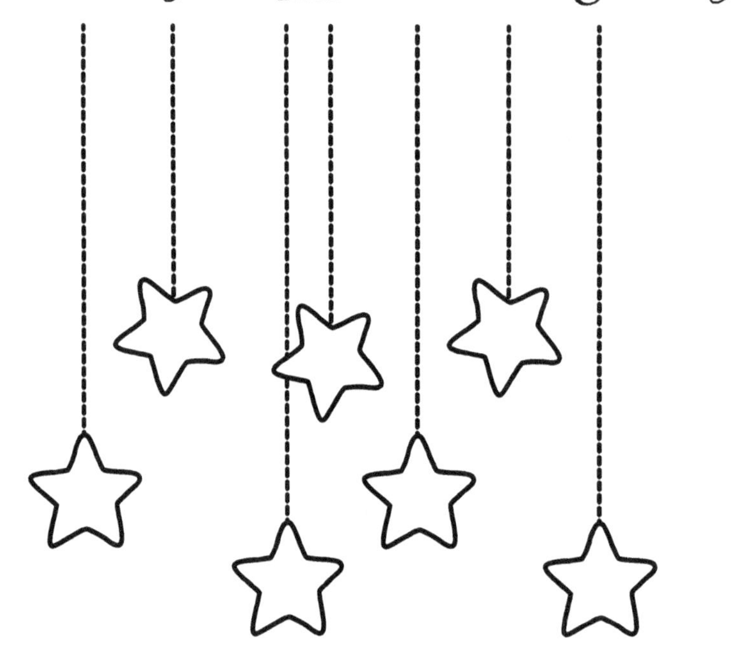

Activity

Find the following hidden words in the grid below
(they could be written in any direction):

sweater, cards, stocking, holiday,
sleigh, frosty, bells, candy, jolly

S T O C K I N G E S
L A K E I V N B S H
P O H Y H C A R D S
R A O K B A K E U L
E L L L H N I B Y E
T L I I Y D B B Y I
A L D G E Y W E P G
E K A S D N C L S H
W O Y Y J O L L Y D
S S F I F R O S T Y

Journal Page

Today

Today Santa helped Elfis Elf get to sleep by reading him a bedtime story. Santa fell asleep as well!

Do you have a favorite Christmas book? If so, what is it called? I have been told that '*Santa's Sleigh is on its Way to My House*' is a very good book indeed. I forget who the author is!

(cough, cough)

I wonder what Santa will get up to tomorrow!

December 21st

On the 21st of December
In the factory, there's much clapping.
They've finished making all the toys,
So now it's time for wrapping!

When the day is over,
And the elves go home to bed,
There's tape stuck to their bottoms
And there's glitter on their heads!

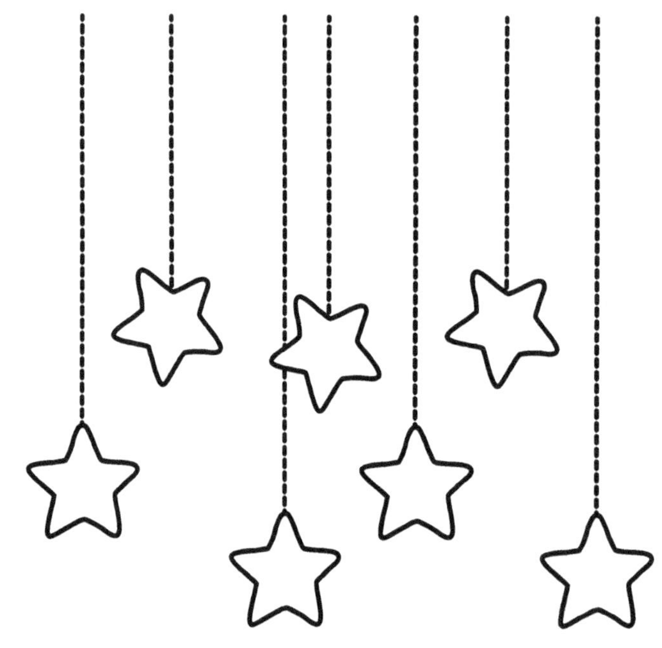

Activity

CHRISTMAS SCRAMBLE 2

Those two cheeky elves have done it again.
They've mixed up *longer words* this time.
Can you unscramble them for me?

You'll find the answers at the back of the book

REEDEIRN

STRIHACMS

SNESETPR

YAHIDOLS

Journal Page

Today

Today the elves finished making all the presents and started to wrap them. They got rather messy. I think that may have been on purpose!

The oldest record we have of a gift being wrapped up dates all the way back to 100 BC in China.

Paper wasn't invented back then, so it's most likely they used bamboo, leaves or cloths.

I wonder what Santa will get up to tomorrow!

December 22nd

On the 22nd of December
There's a party for the elves.
Santa says that once again
They've all outdone themselves.

They eat delicious Christmas snacks
And dance the night away.
Santa gives them presents
To unwrap on Christmas Day!

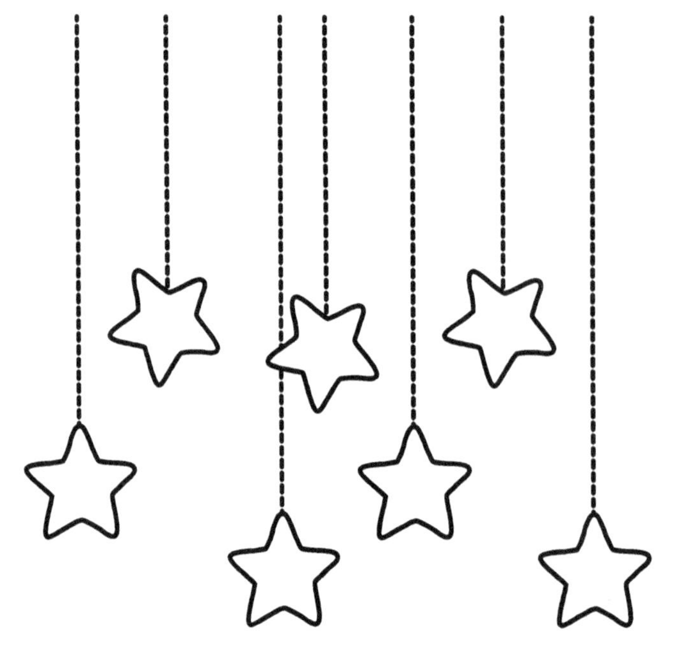

Activity

Why not put on a little play for your family?

Act out what happens on Christmas morning when everyone receives their presents. Imagine what happens if all of the presents get mixed up. Would anyone make funny sounds or funny faces if they got something they weren't expecting?

You could even create posters to advertise your play, and give it a fun name like 'Crazy Christmas'. Don't forget to send me an invite to the opening night!

Journal Page

Today

Today Santa held a party for the elves to thank them for all their hard work.

Did you get to go to any Christmas parties this year? If so, did you remember to write about them in your journal?

I wonder what Santa will get up to tomorrow!

December 23rd

On the 23rd of December
Santa bakes a carrot pie.
He takes it to the reindeer
As a treat before they fly.

'Eat up! You'll need your energy
to fly right through the night.
We've made so many toys this year
The sleigh will not be light!'

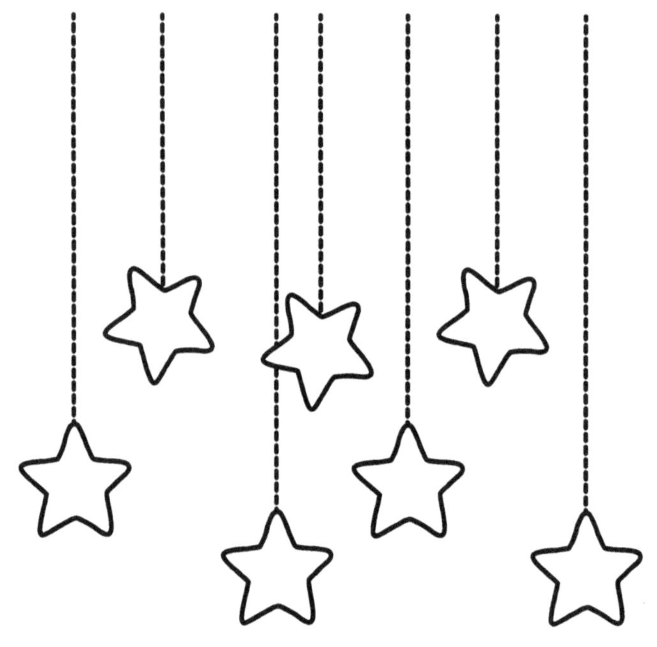

Activity

Color this picture of Santa!

I've not put anything important on this page.
that's because it follows a coloring activity.
If the colors show through the paper, it won't
matter as much :)

Parents: this occasionally means a slight tweak
to the order in which the pages appear.

Journal Page

Today

Today Santa made a delicious carrot pie for the reindeer.

Reindeer occasionally enjoy treats like apples, carrots and other fruits, but they mainly eat mosses, herbs, ferns, grasses and the leaves of shrubs and trees.

They even have a plant-like organism named after them: Reindeer lichen.

I wonder what Santa will get up to tomorrow!

December 24th

On the 24th of December
Santa's loading up his sleigh.
This is the part he loves the most.
This is his FAVORITE day!

He pats down all the reindeer,
Gives the village one last wave.
He booms out ....

'MERRY CHRISTMAS '

Then he shouts

'UP, UP, AWAY!'

Activity

Help Santa find his way down the crazy chimney
(The answer is at the back of the book)

Journal Page

Today

It's Christmas Eve and Santa finally takes off on his sleigh!

Do you get much sleep the night before Christmas
or are you usually TOO EXCITED?!

I think Santa might have a day off tomorrow!

December 25th

It's the 25th of December!
There's one thing left to say:

I hope you have a
BRILLIANT
WONDERFUL
MAGICAL

CHRISTMAS DAY!!!

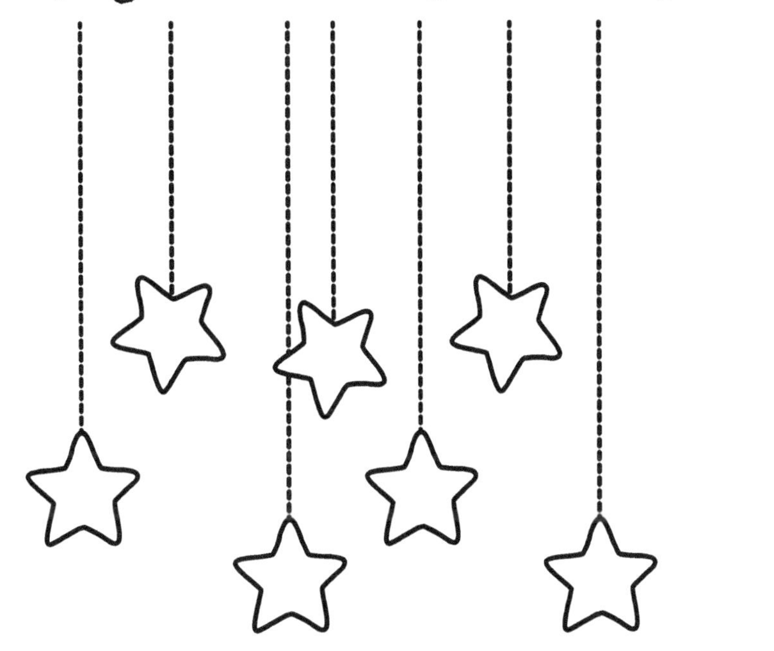

Journal Page

Journal Page

Journal Page

Enjoyed this journal?

Visit this author's website for more

ericjames.co.uk

Answers

Did you get stuck on any of the puzzles? The following pages contain the answers!

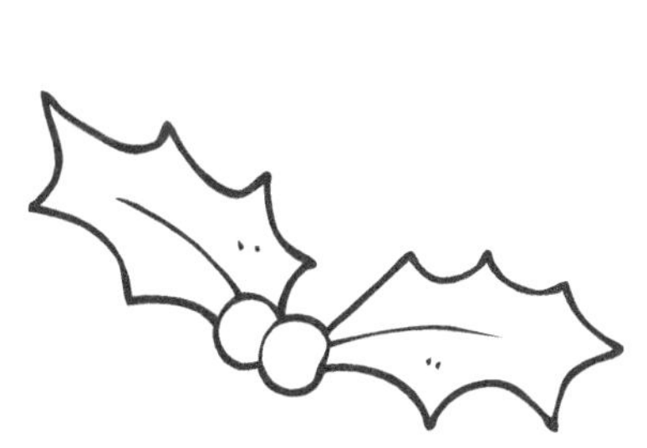

Answers

CHRISTMAS SCRAMBLE 1

Santa, Tree, Gifts, Snow

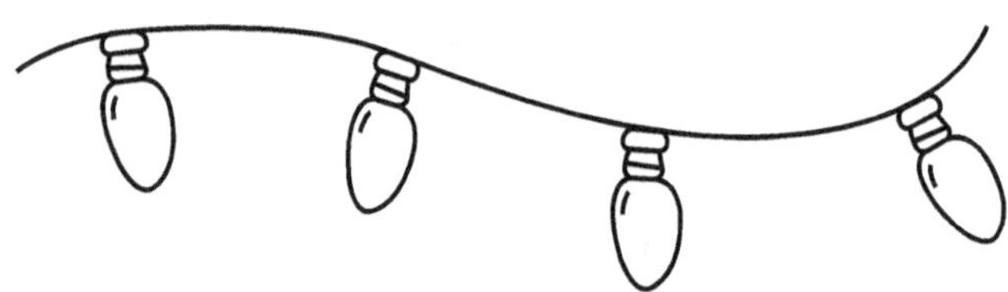

CHRISTMAS SCRAMBLE 2

Reindeer, Christmas, Presents, Holidays

Answers

PENGUIN MAZE

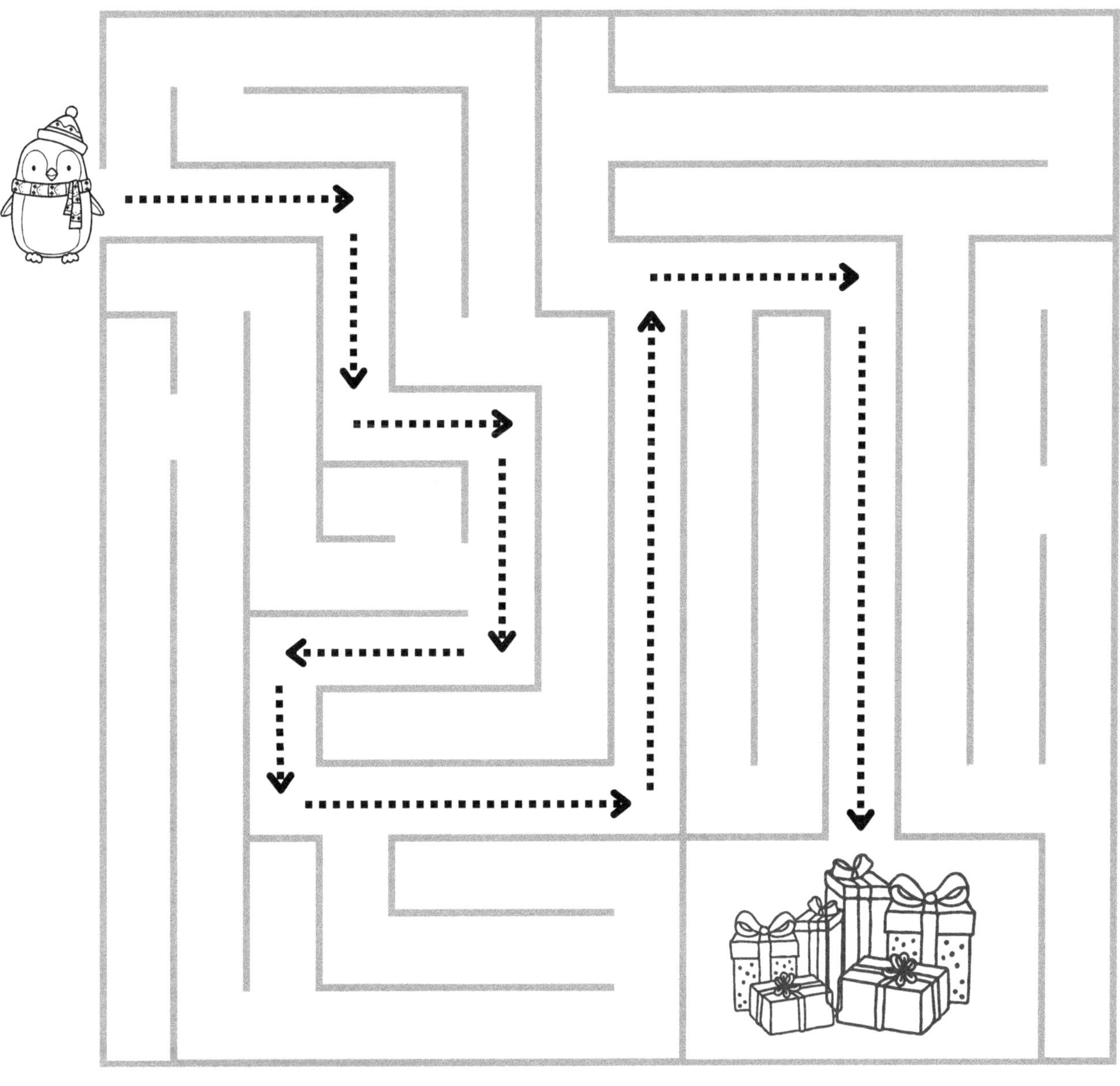

Answers

WORD SEARCH 1

santa, snowball, penguins, ginger, present, ice, snowflake, scarf, tree

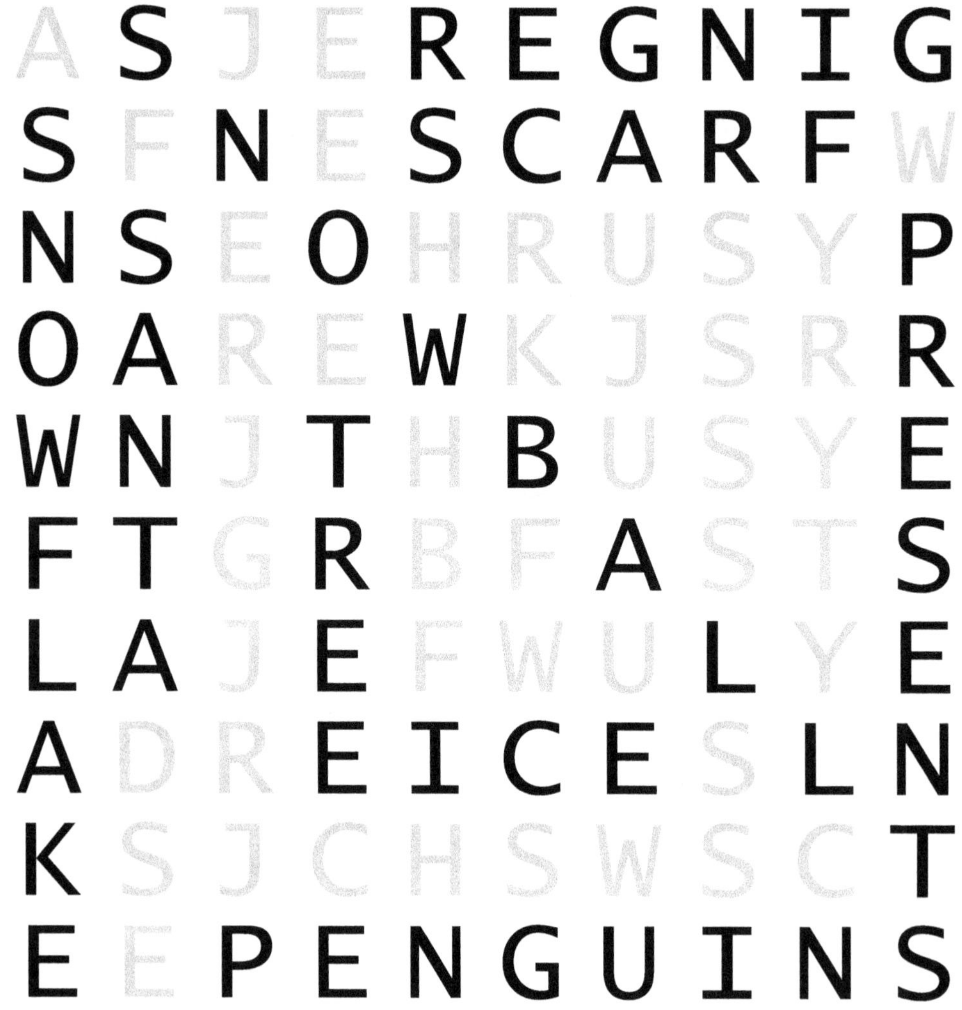

Answers

SPOT THE DIFFERENCE 1

There are 5 differences between the pictures:

Answers

CHRISTMAS QUIZ

Q1:

How many reindeer does Santa have?

9

Q2:

Where does Santa live?

The North Pole (you can also say Lapland)

Q3:

What color is the Grinch?

Green

Q4:

What is Rudolf's favorite food?

Carrots

Q5:

What type of calendar do we use to count down to Christmas?

An Advent Calendar

Answers

SPOT THE DIFFERENCE 2

There are 5 differences between the pictures:

Answers

WORD SEARCH 2

sweater, cards, stocking, holiday, sleigh, frosty, bells, candy, jolly

Answers

CRAZY CHIMNEY

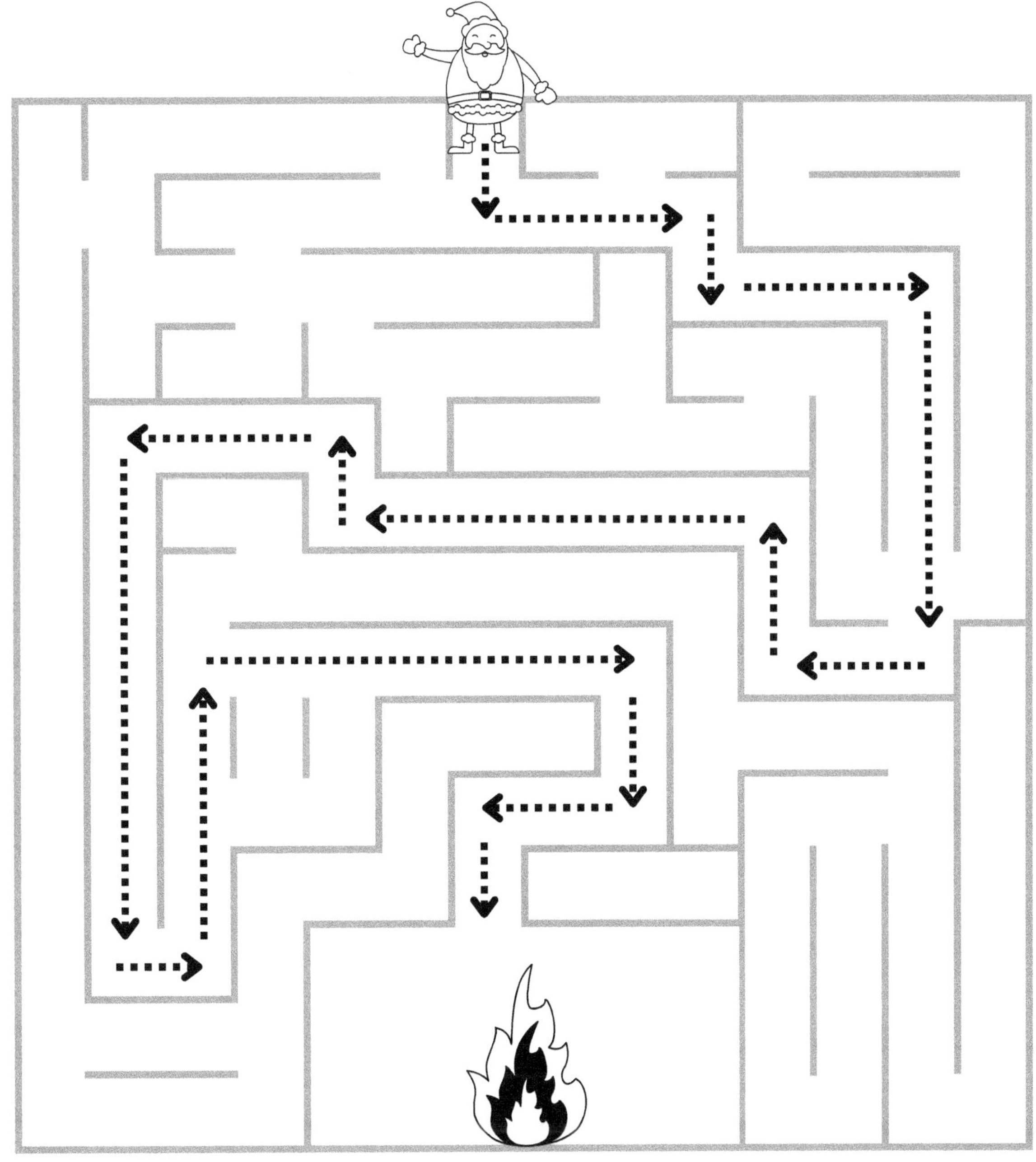

www.ingramcontent.com/pod-product-compliance
Lightning Source LLC
LaVergne TN
LVHW060823170826
845678LV00010B/1881

9781916990081